AF261526

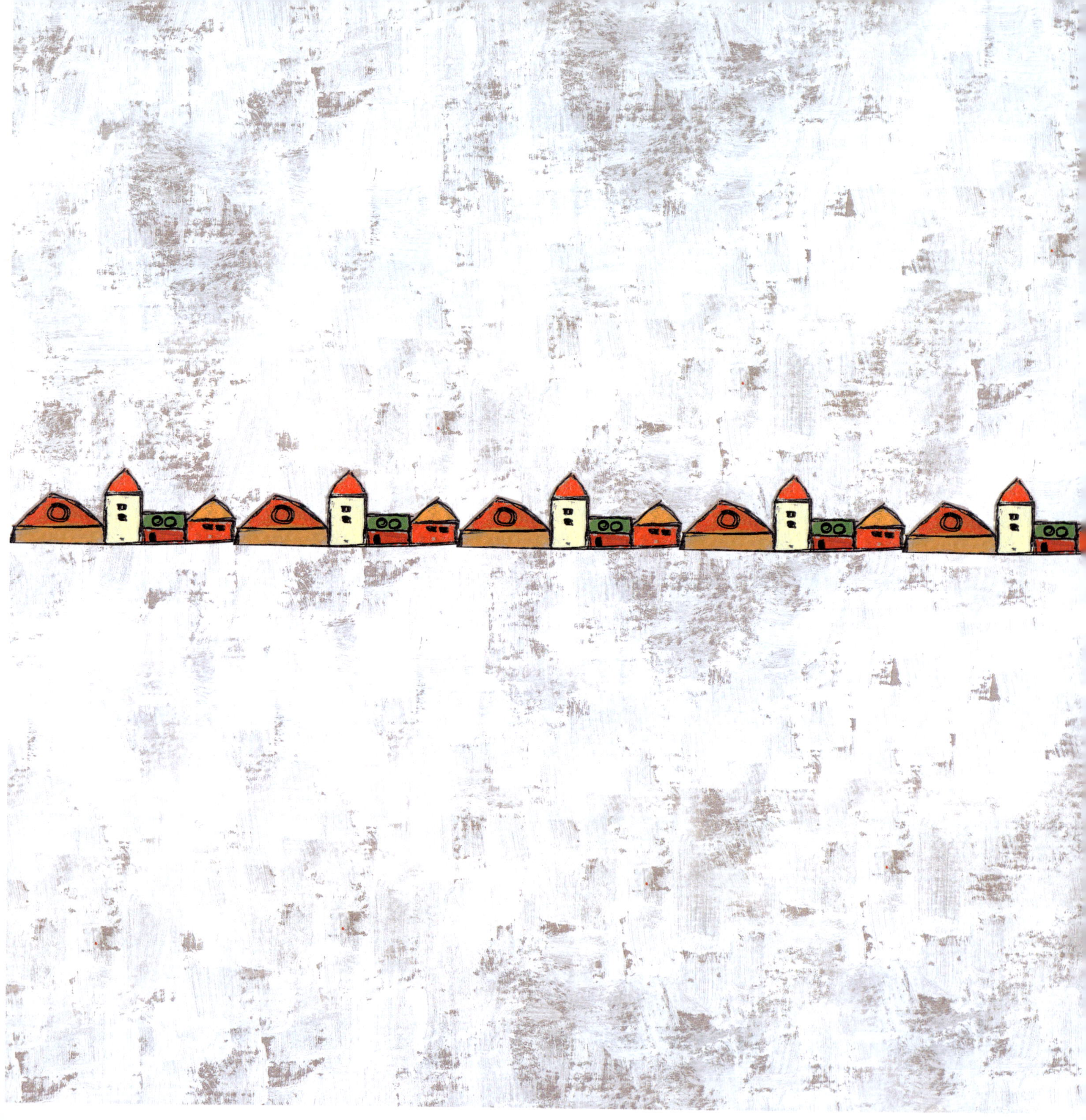

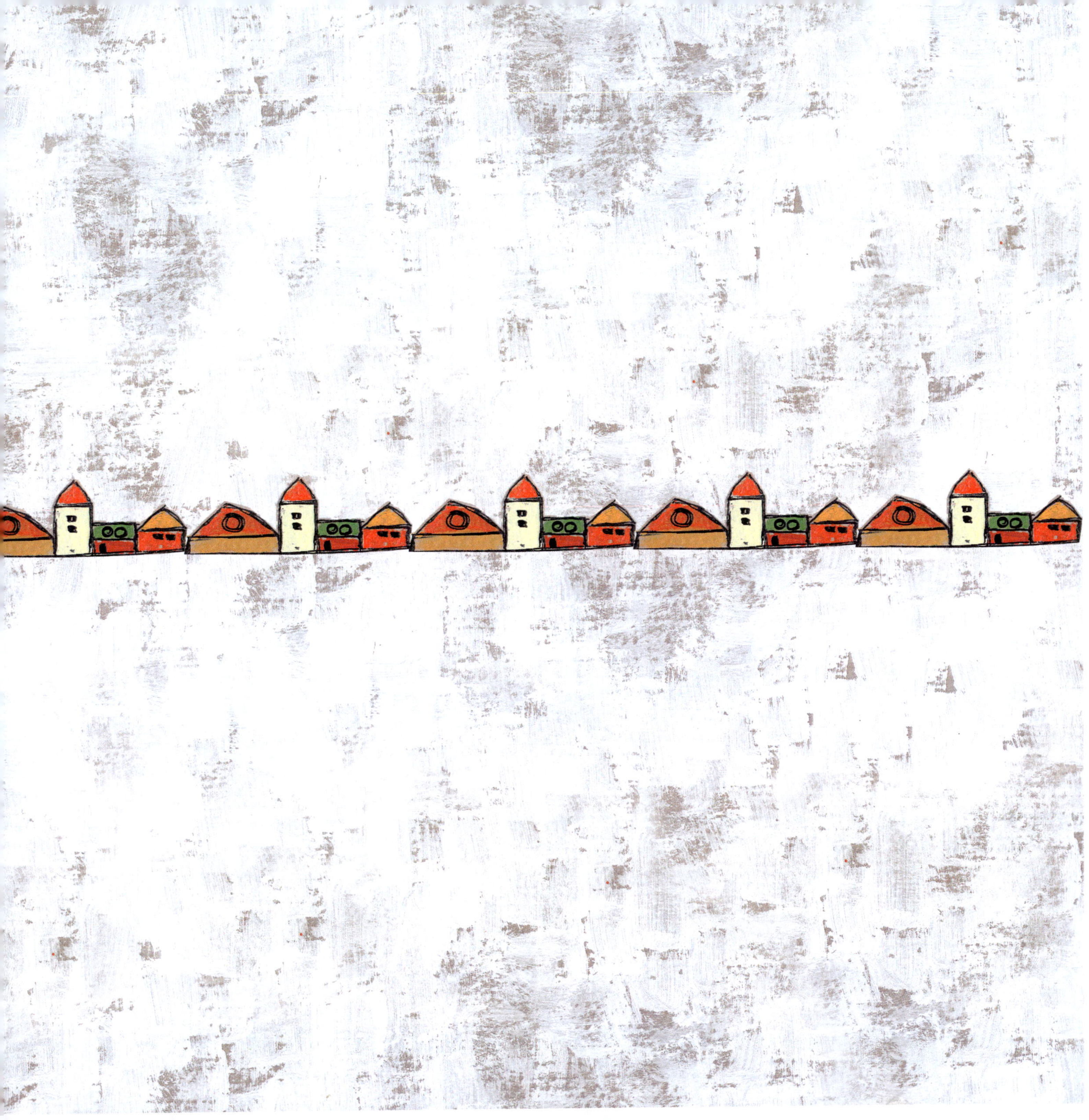

# THE COBBLER

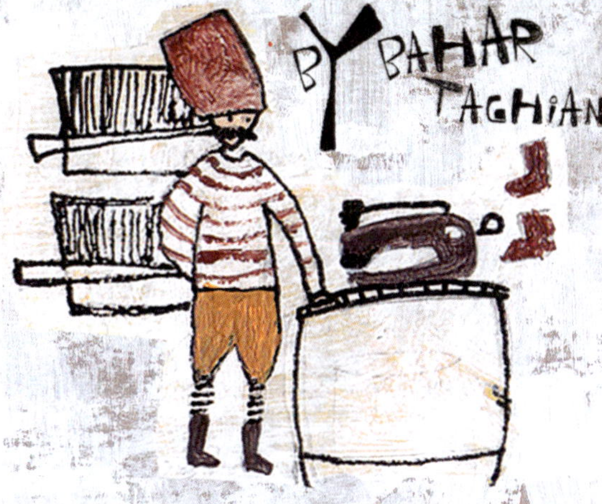

BY BAHAR TAGHIANI

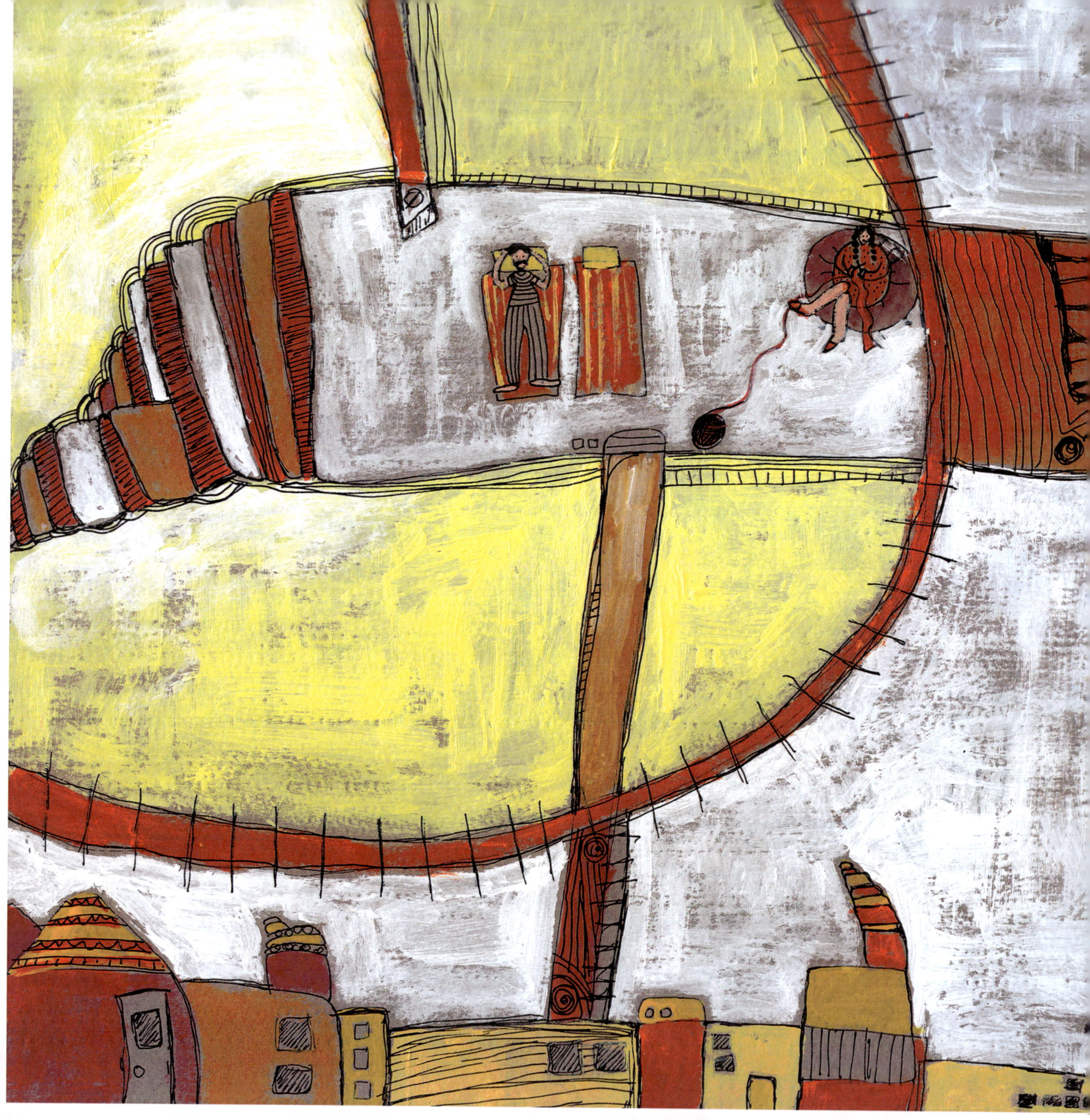

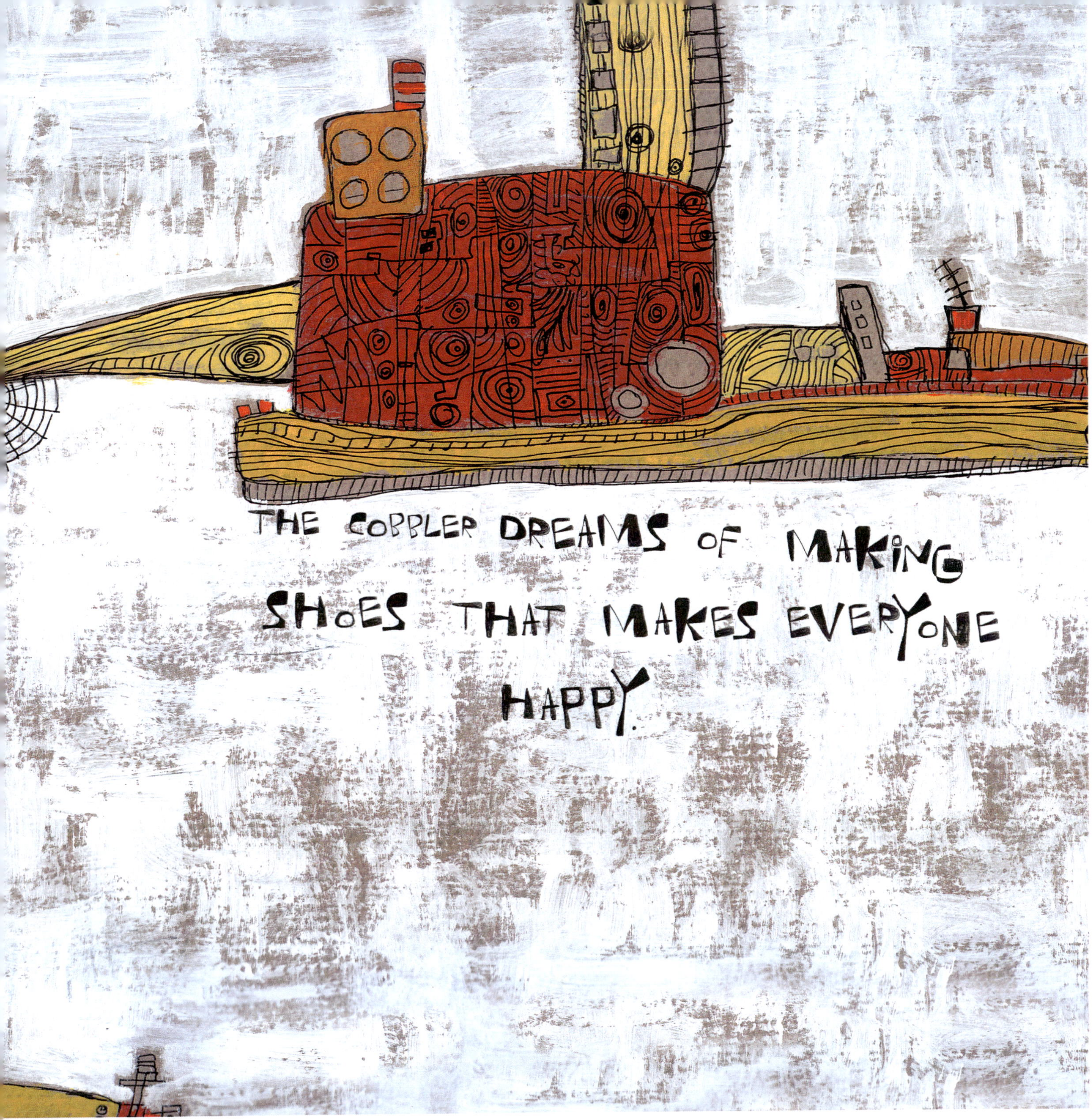

THE COBBLER DREAMS OF MAKING
SHOES THAT MAKES EVERYONE
HAPPY.

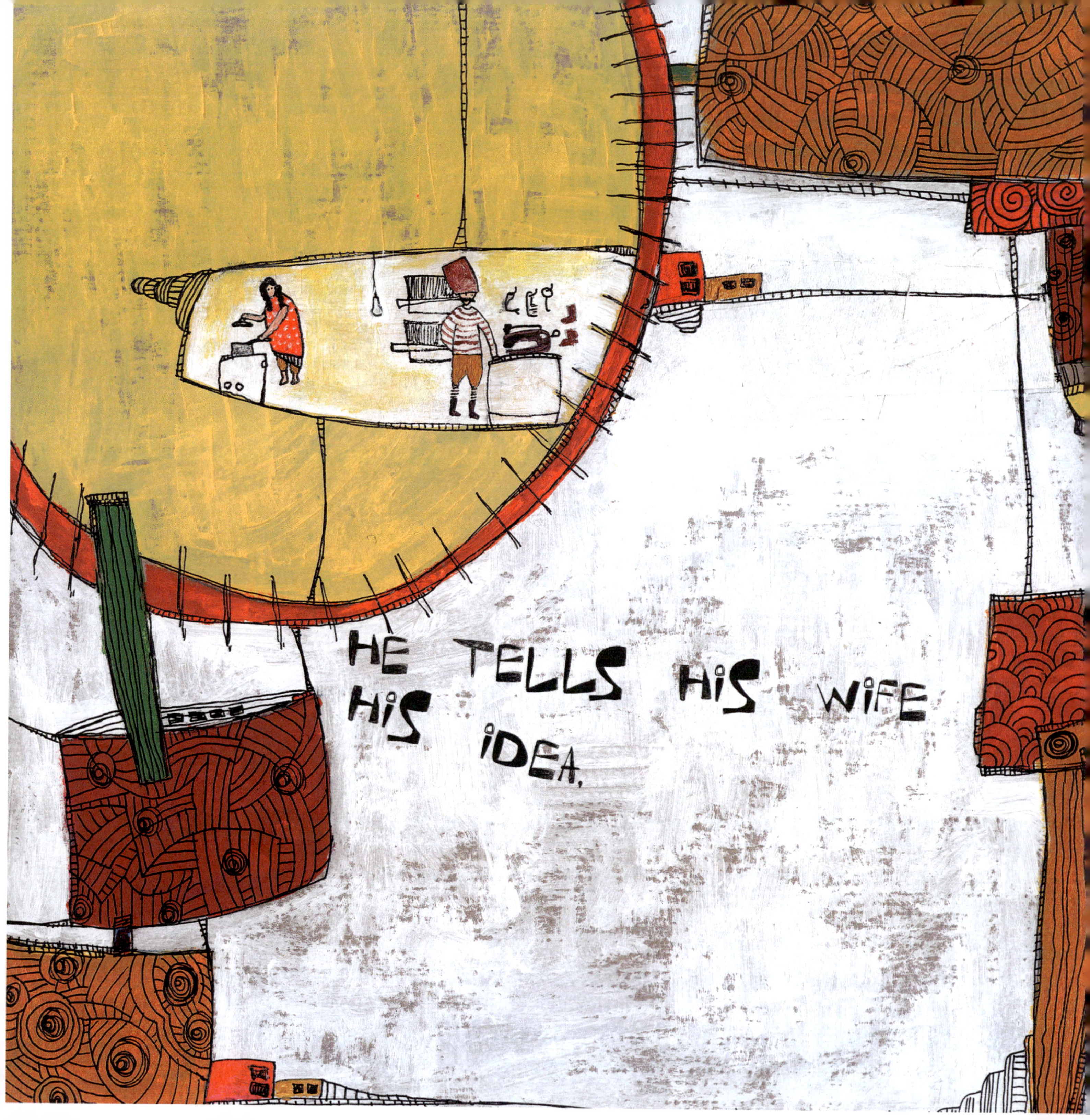

HE TELLS HIS HIS WIFE
HIS IDEA.

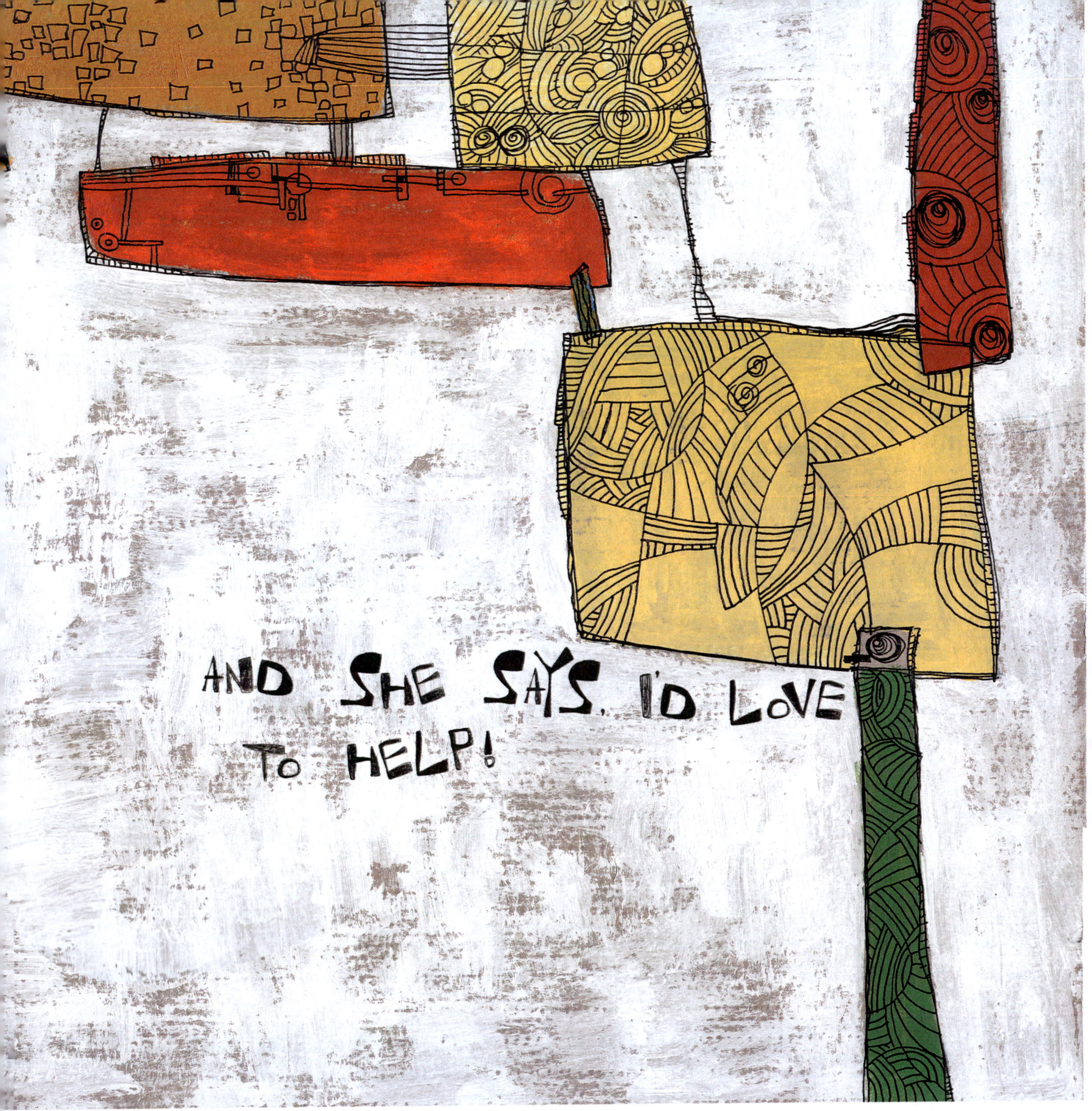
AND SHE SAYS, I'D LOVE
TO HELP!

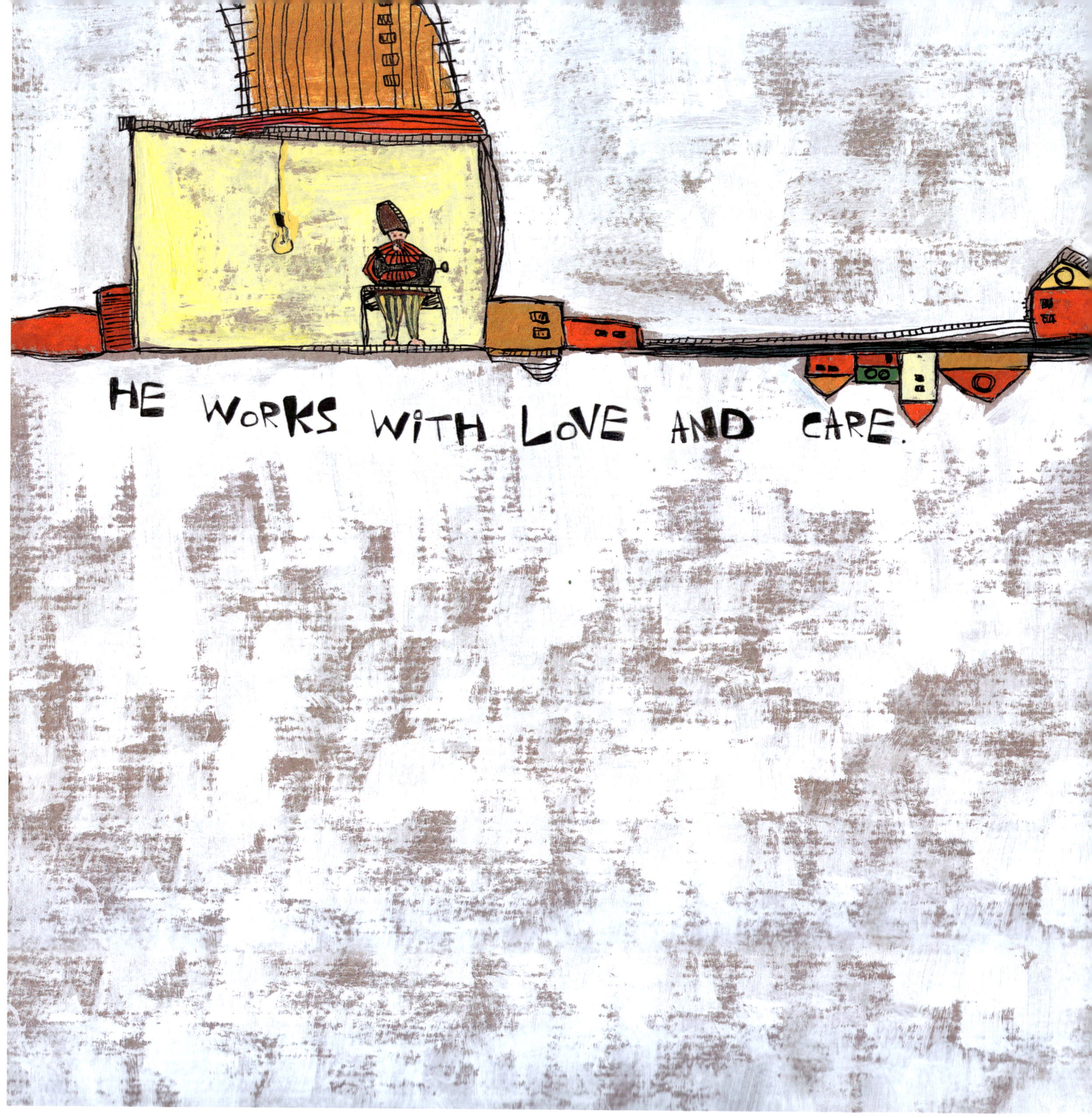

HE WORKS WITH LOVE AND CARE.

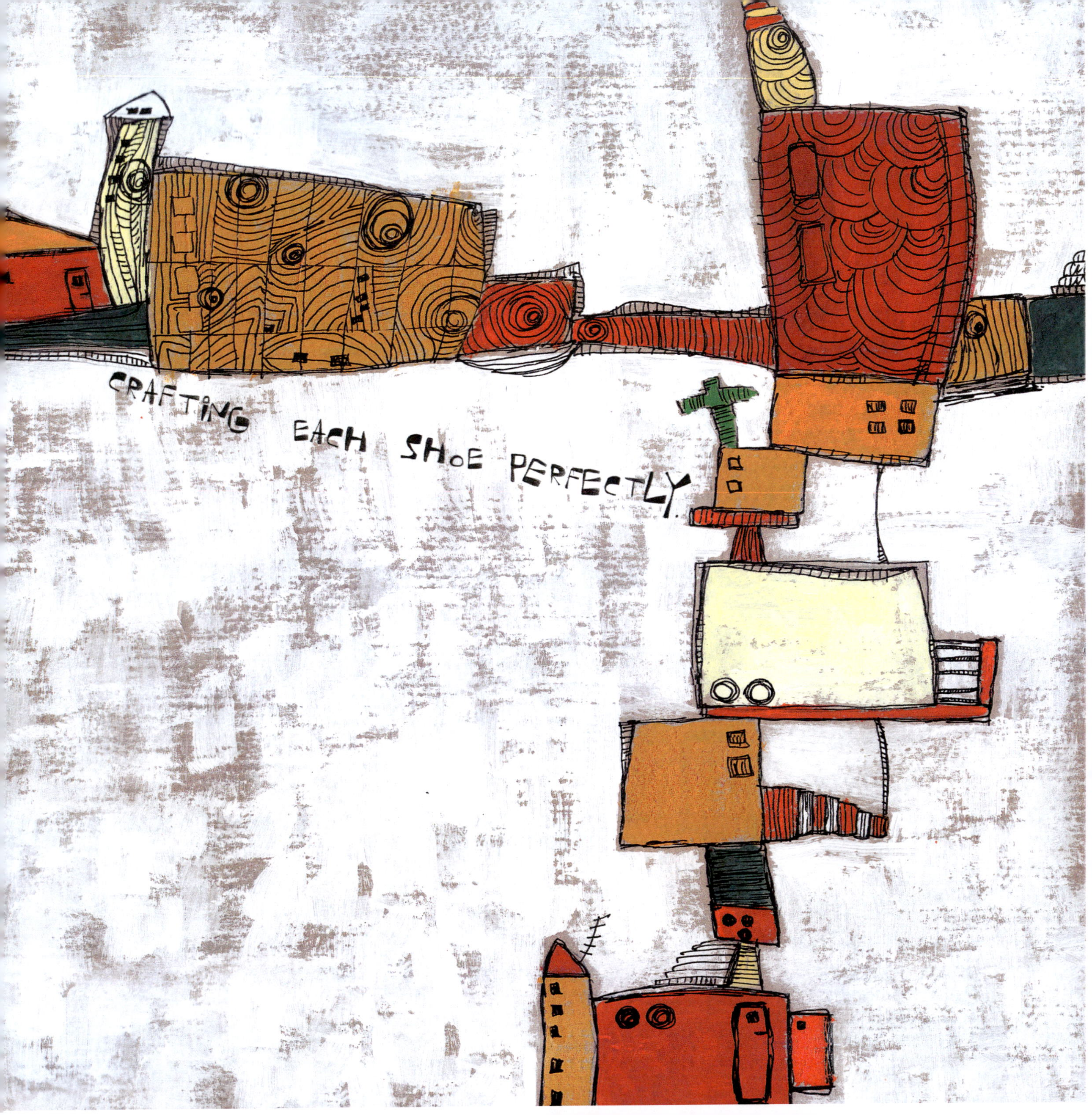
CRAFTING EACH SHOE PERFECTLY.

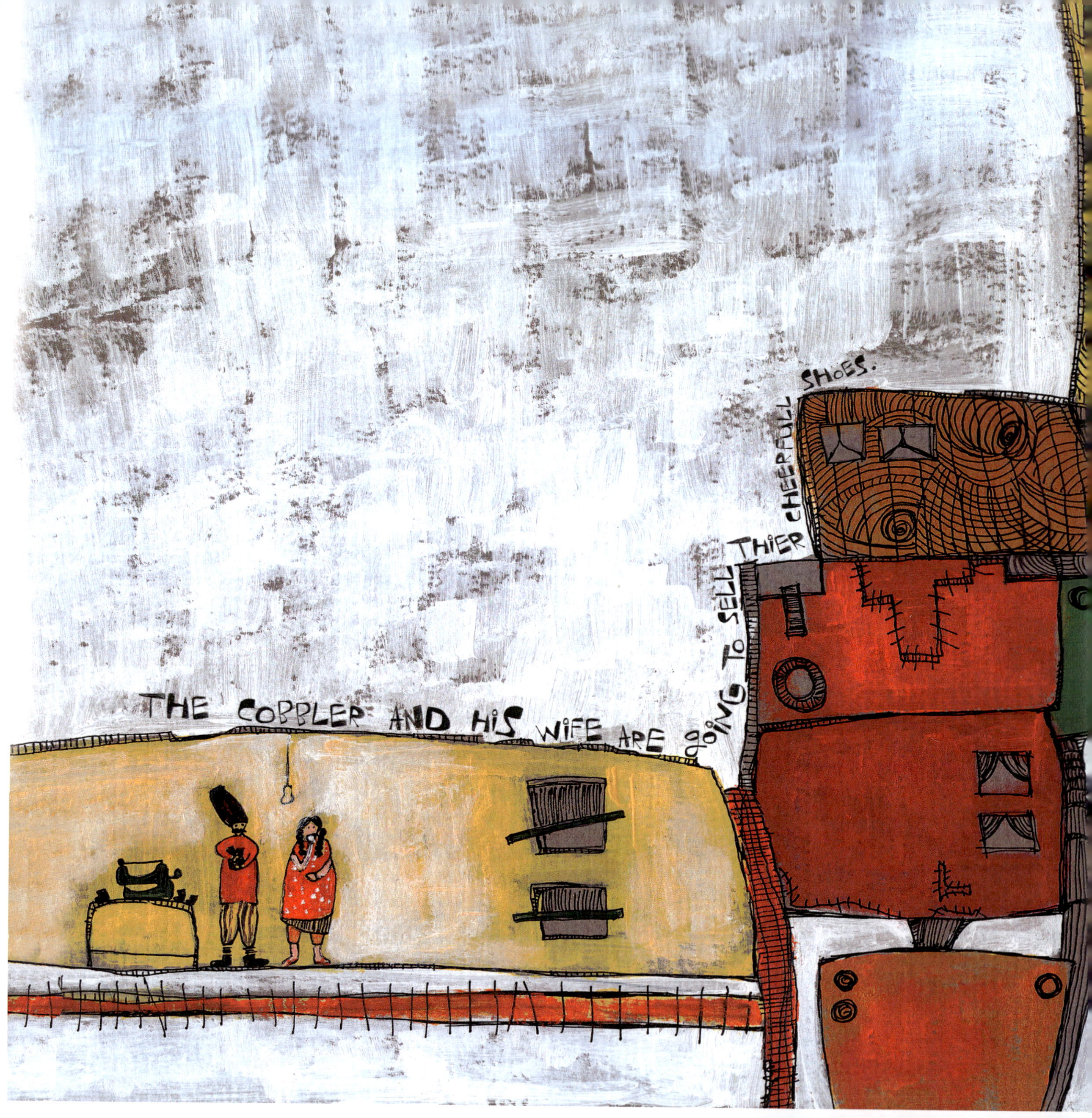

THE COBBLER AND HIS WIFE ARE GOING TO SELL THIER CHEERFULL SHOES.

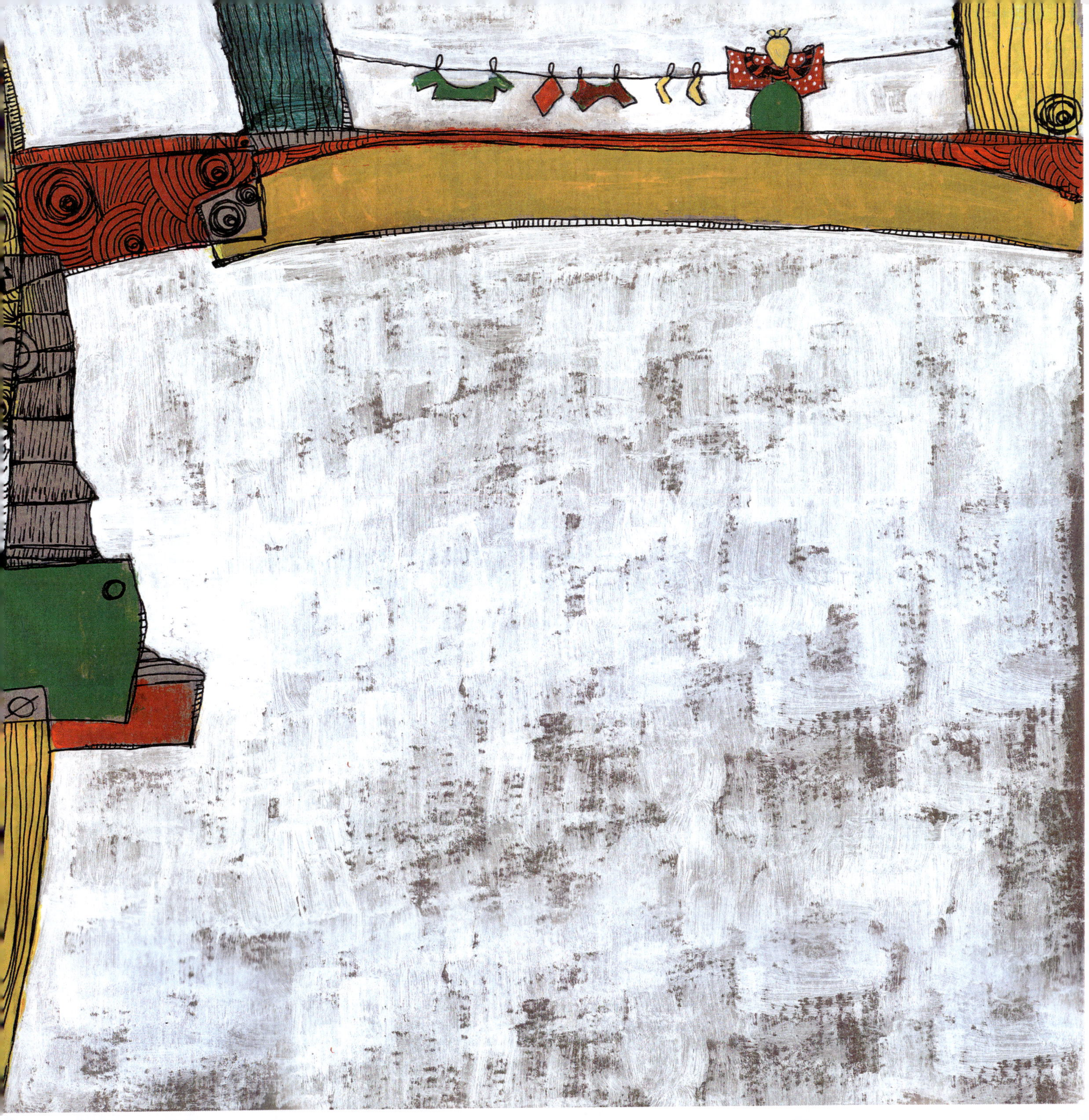

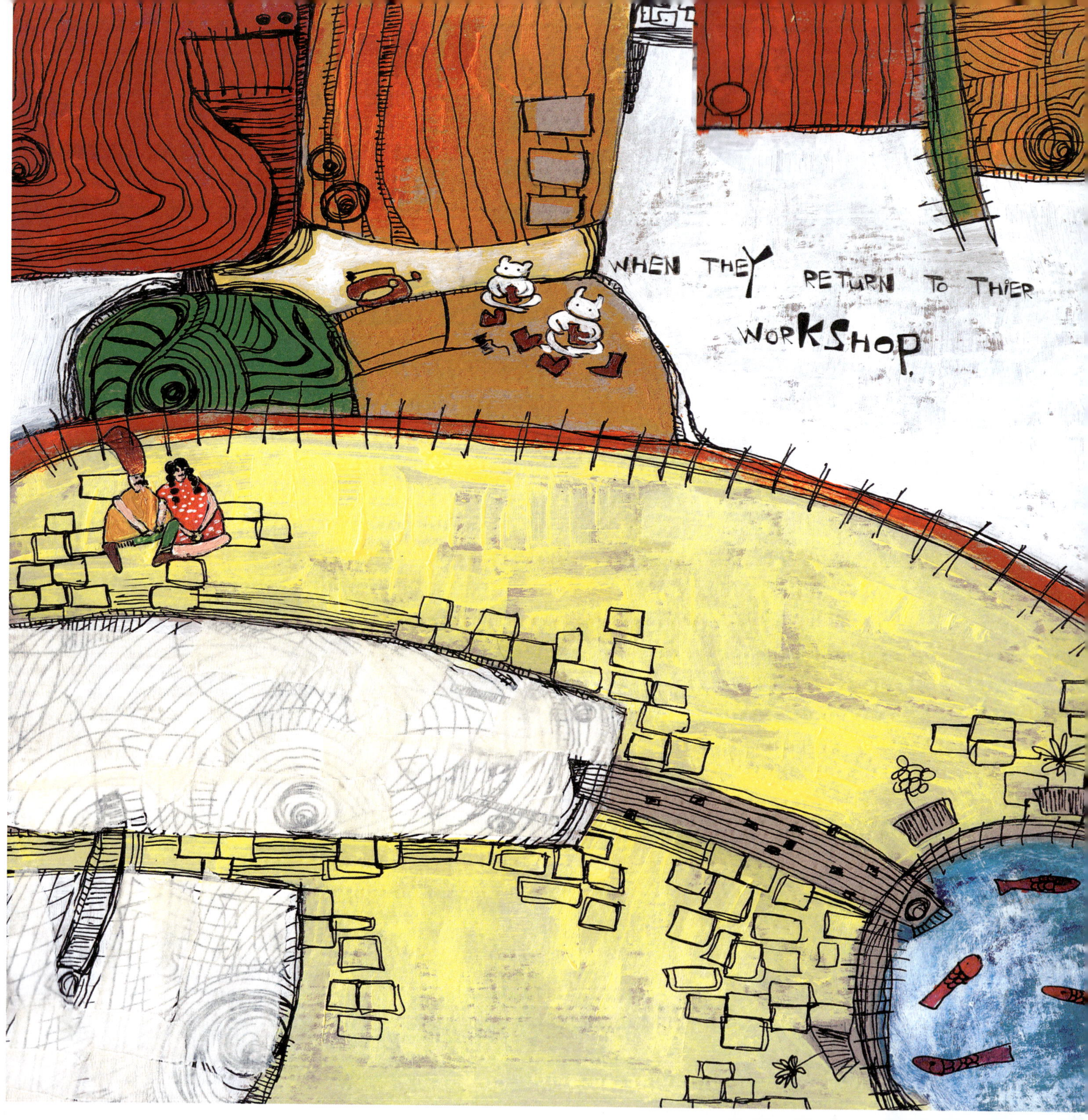

WHEN THEY RETURN TO THIER
WORKSHOP.

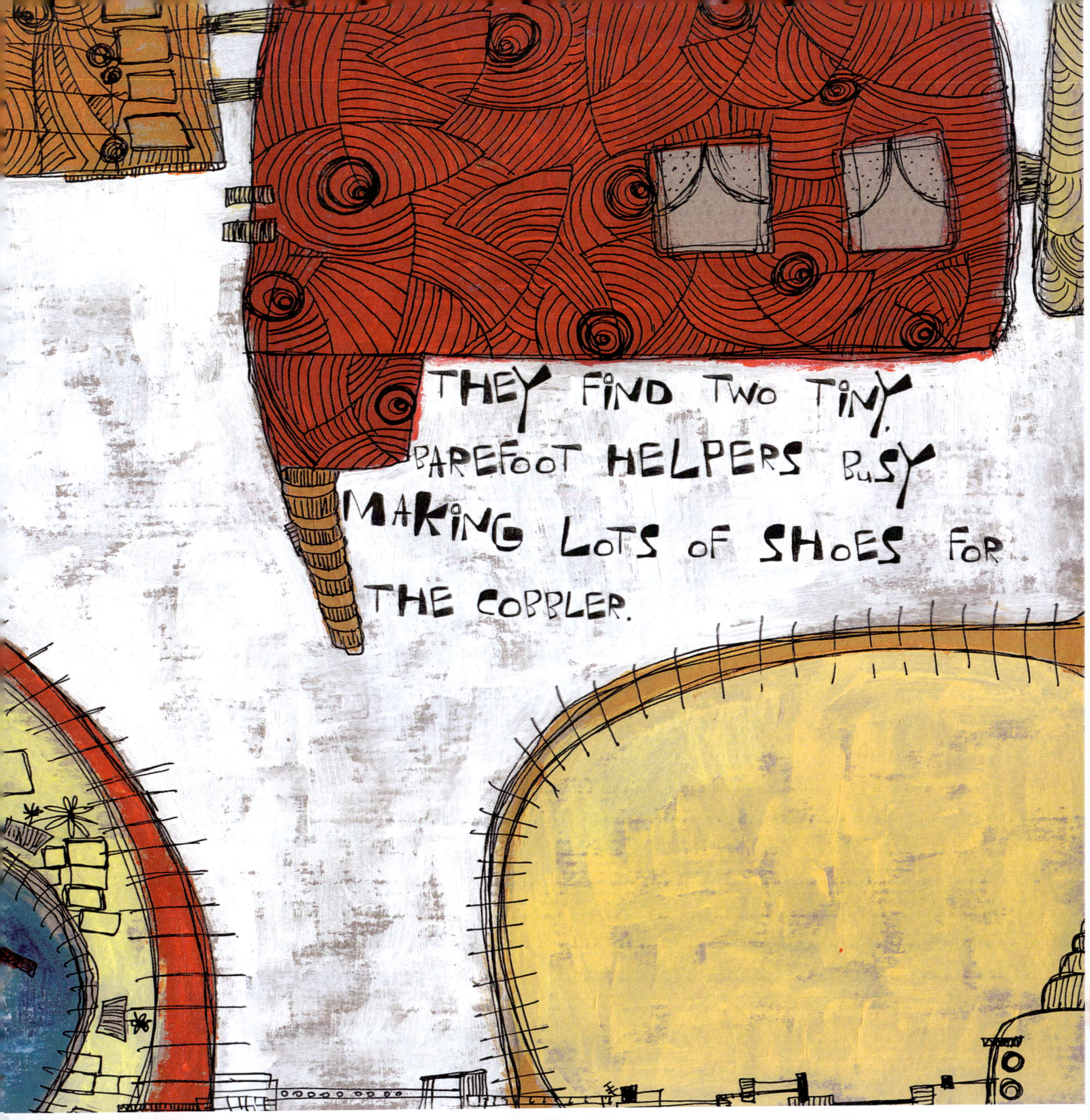
THEY FIND TWO TINY,
BAREFOOT HELPERS BUSY
MAKING LOTS OF SHOES FOR
THE COBBLER.

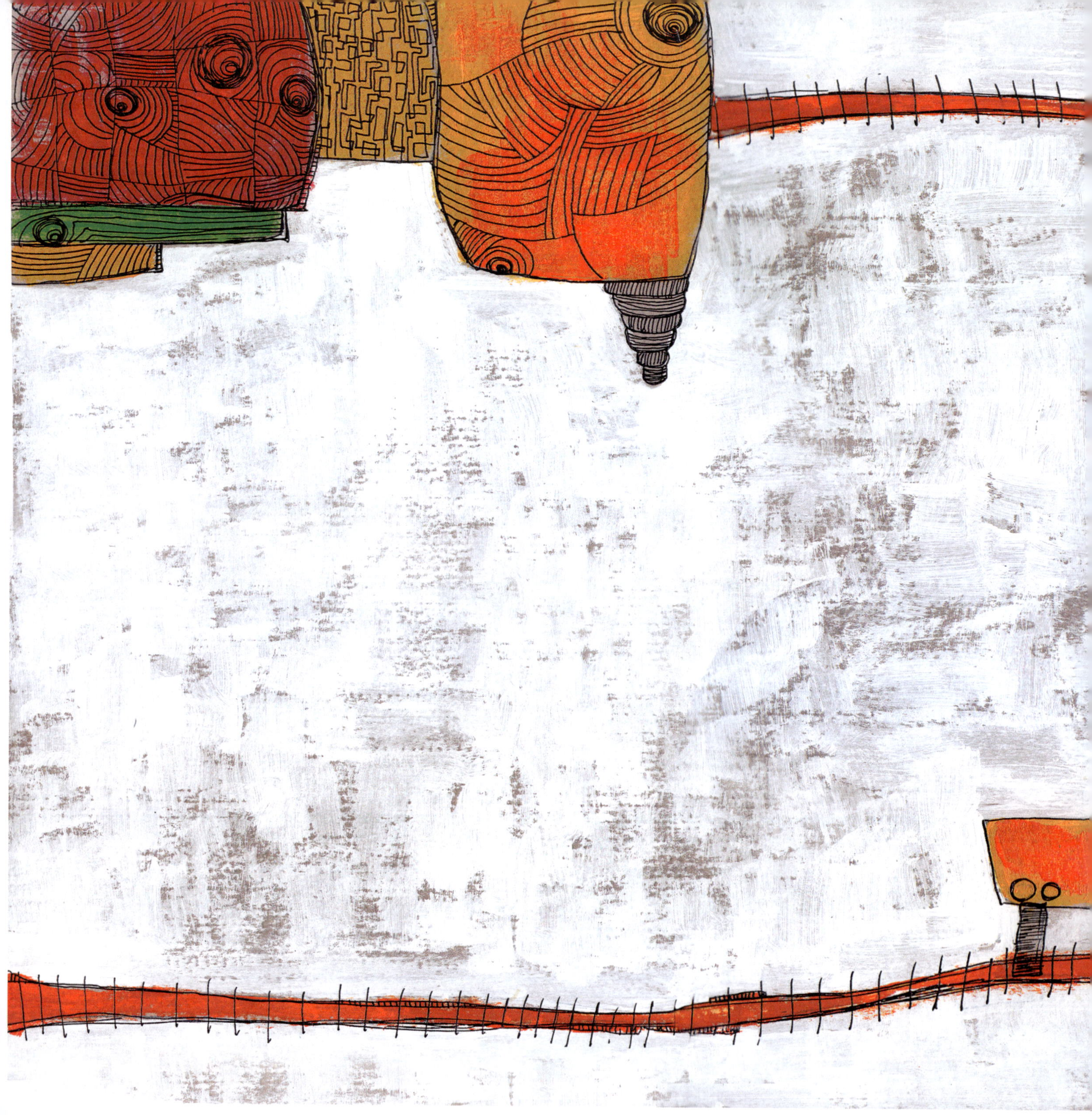

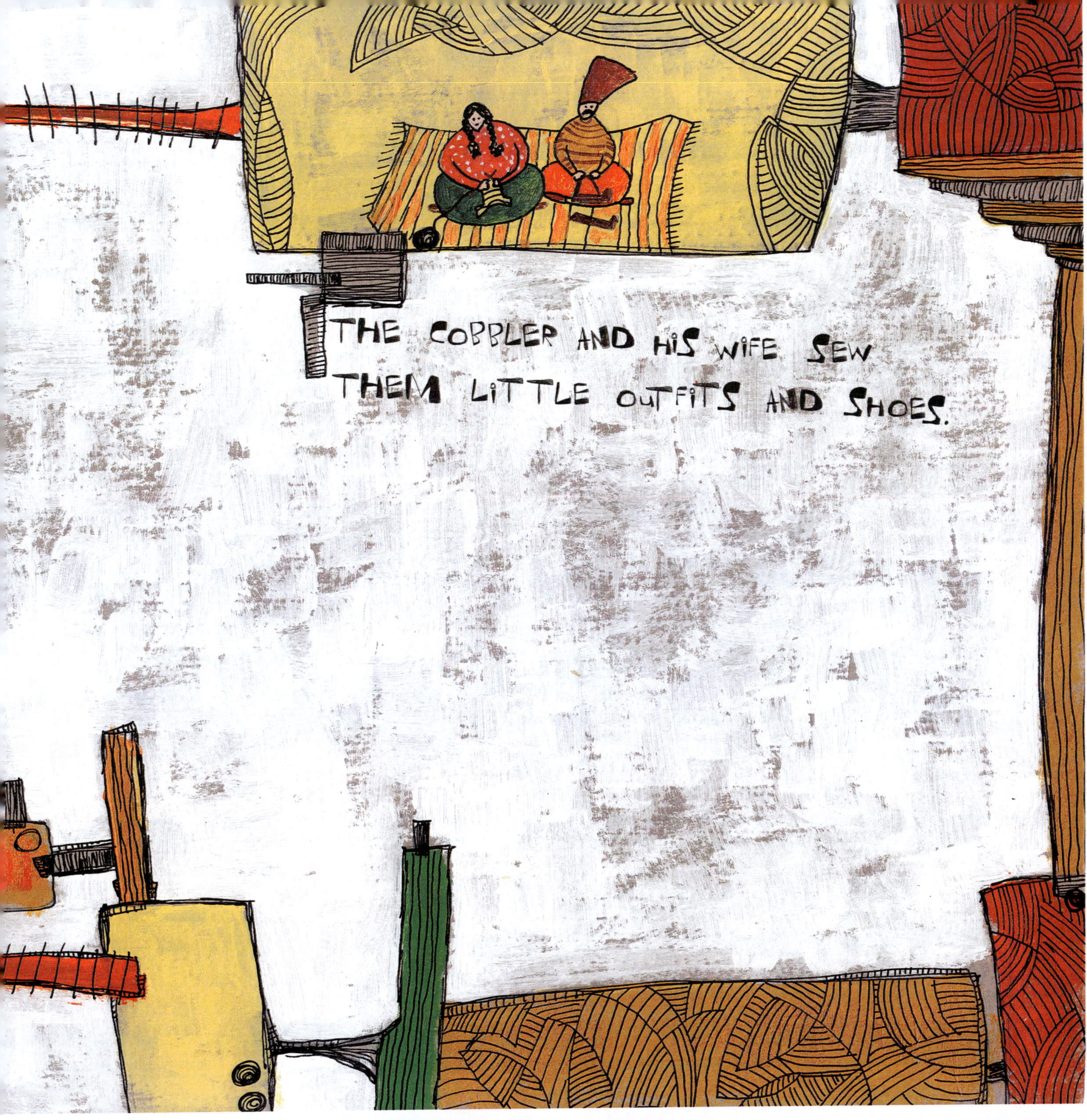

THE COBBLER AND HIS WIFE SEW
THEM LITTLE OUTFITS AND SHOES.

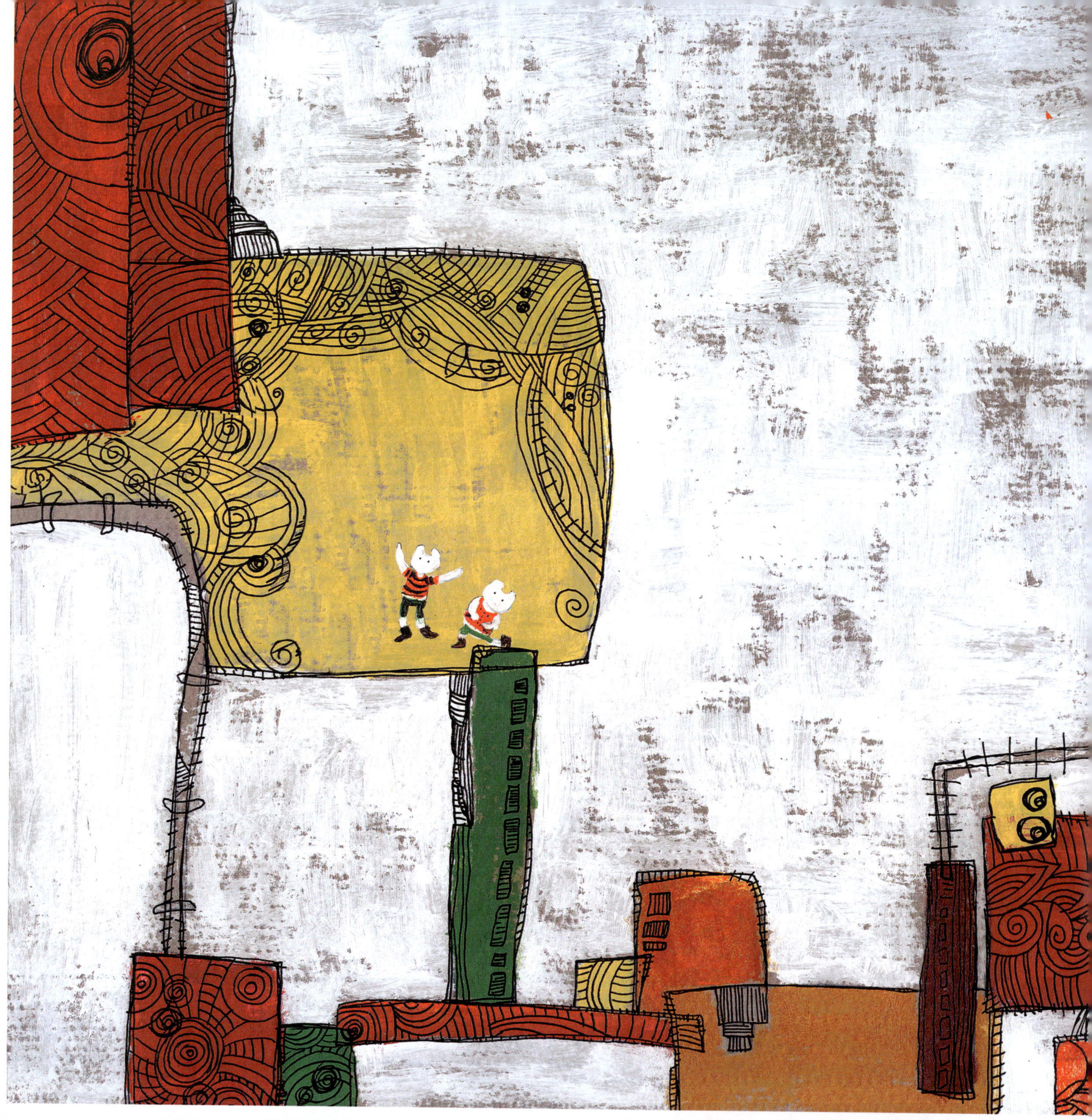

THE TINY HELPERS AND THE VILLAGERS ARE ALL SO HAPPY WITH THE COBBLERS CHEERFULL SHOES.

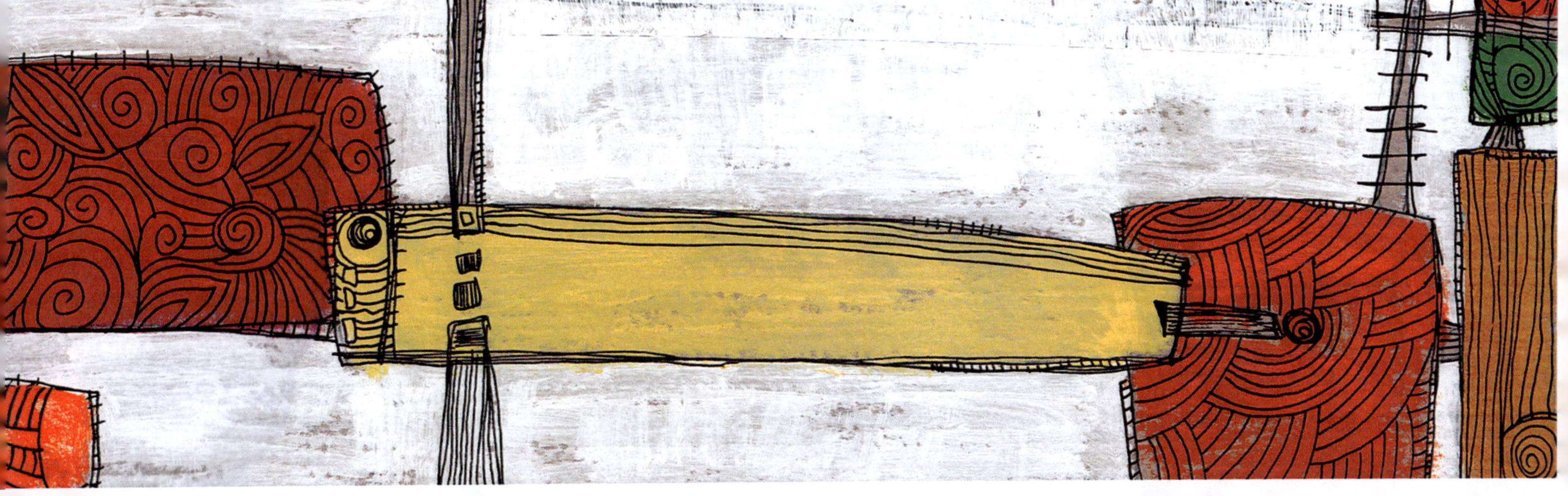

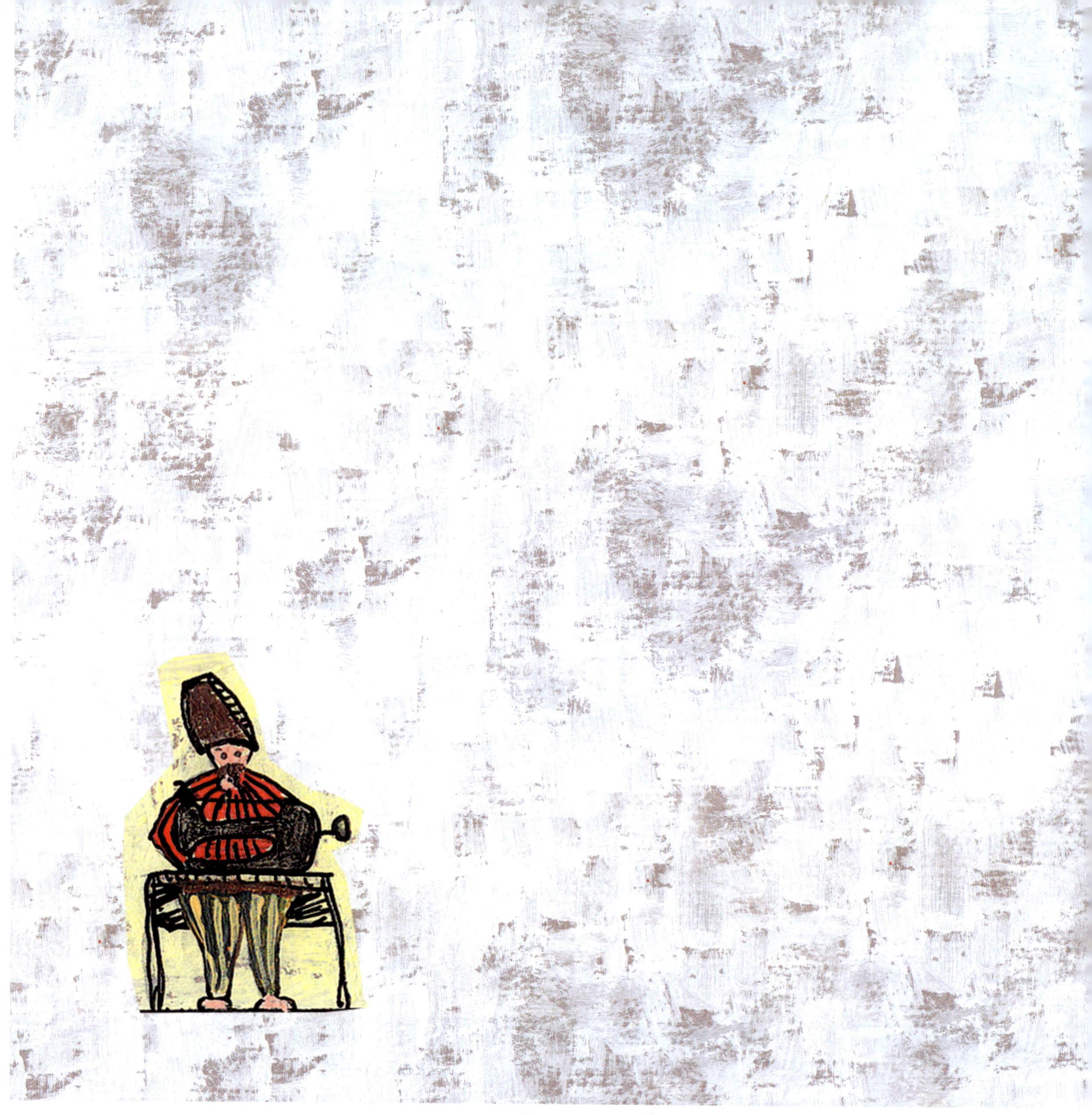

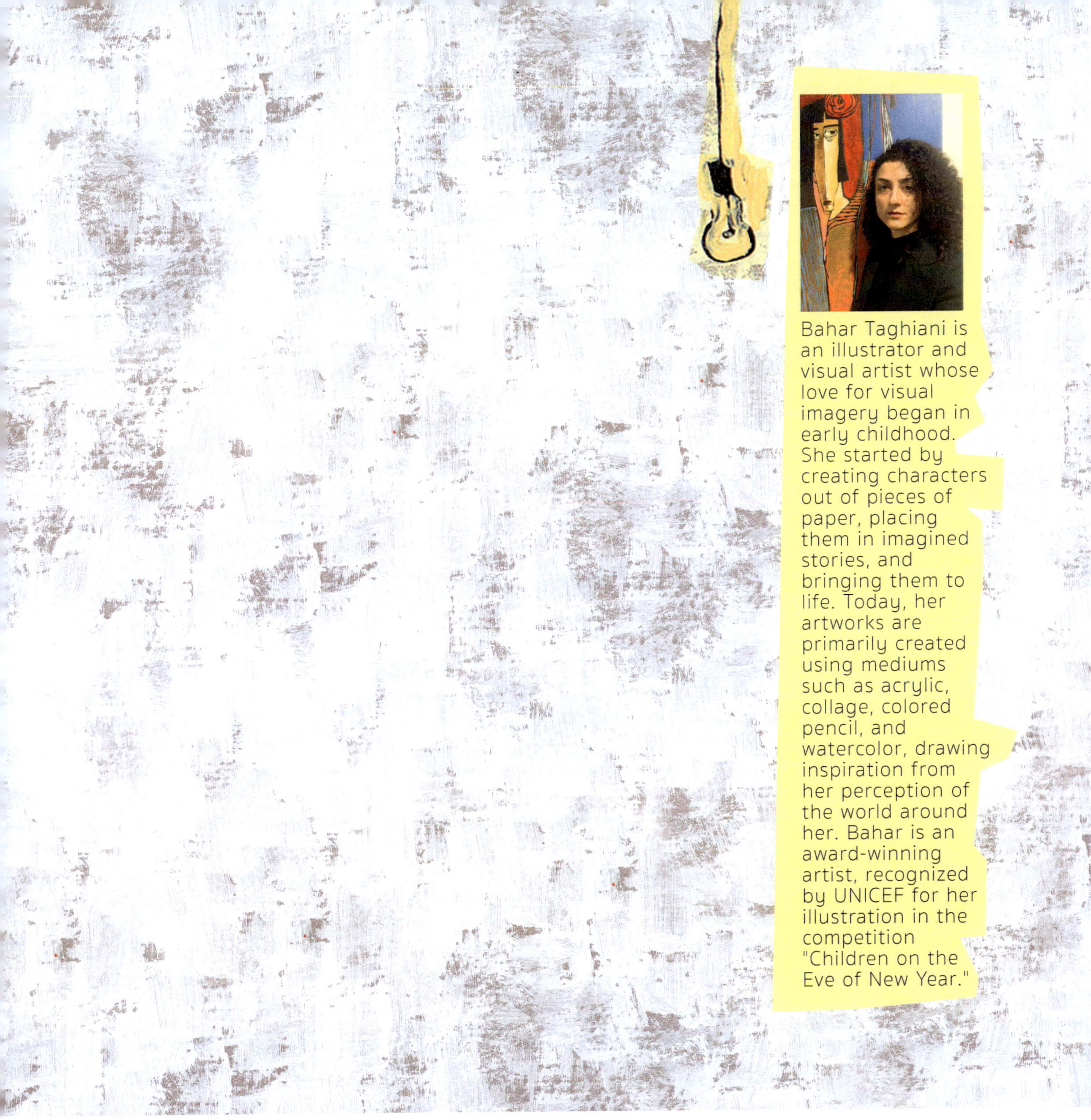

Bahar Taghiani is an illustrator and visual artist whose love for visual imagery began in early childhood. She started by creating characters out of pieces of paper, placing them in imagined stories, and bringing them to life. Today, her artworks are primarily created using mediums such as acrylic, collage, colored pencil, and watercolor, drawing inspiration from her perception of the world around her. Bahar is an award-winning artist, recognized by UNICEF for her illustration in the competition "Children on the Eve of New Year."

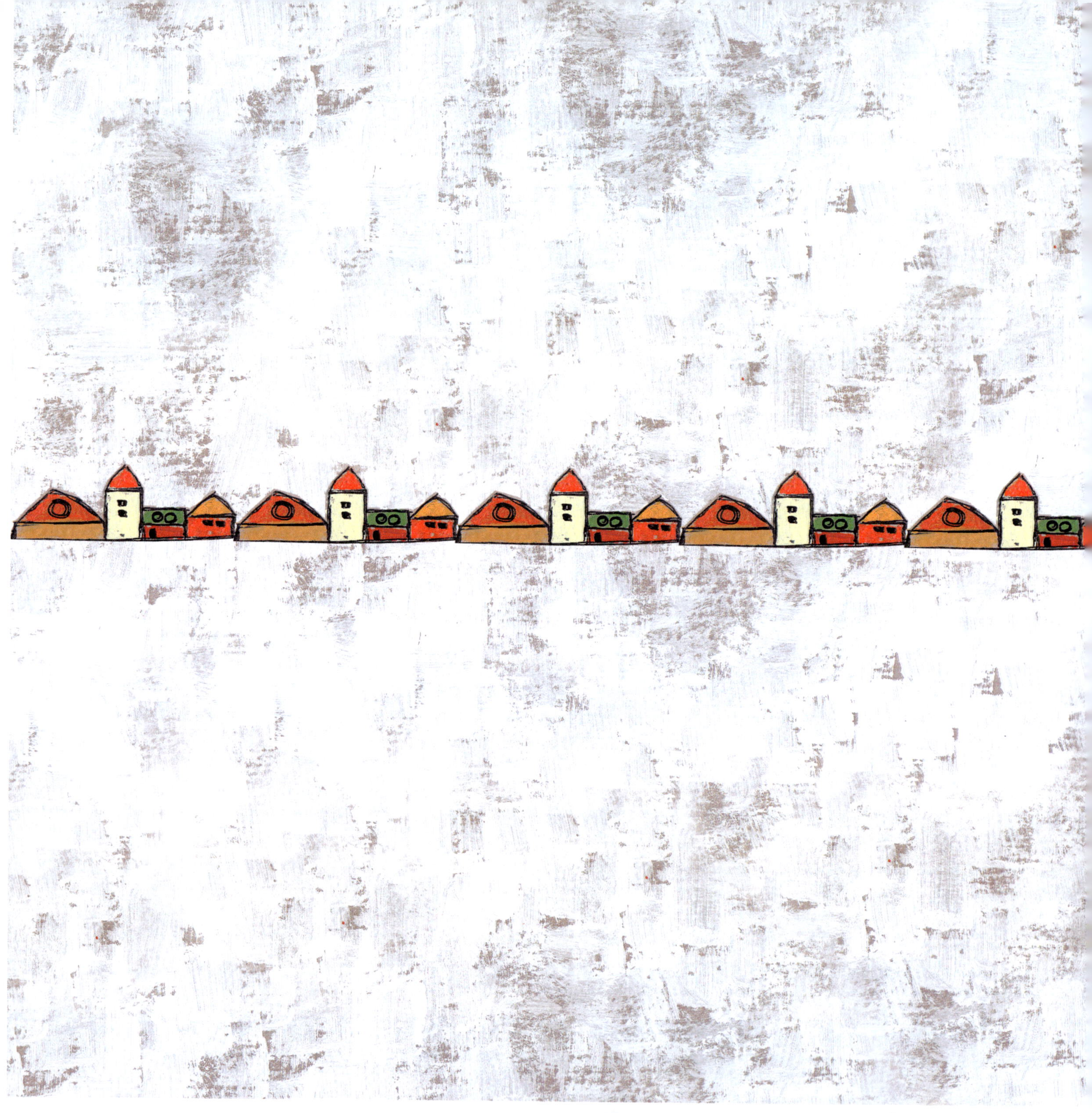

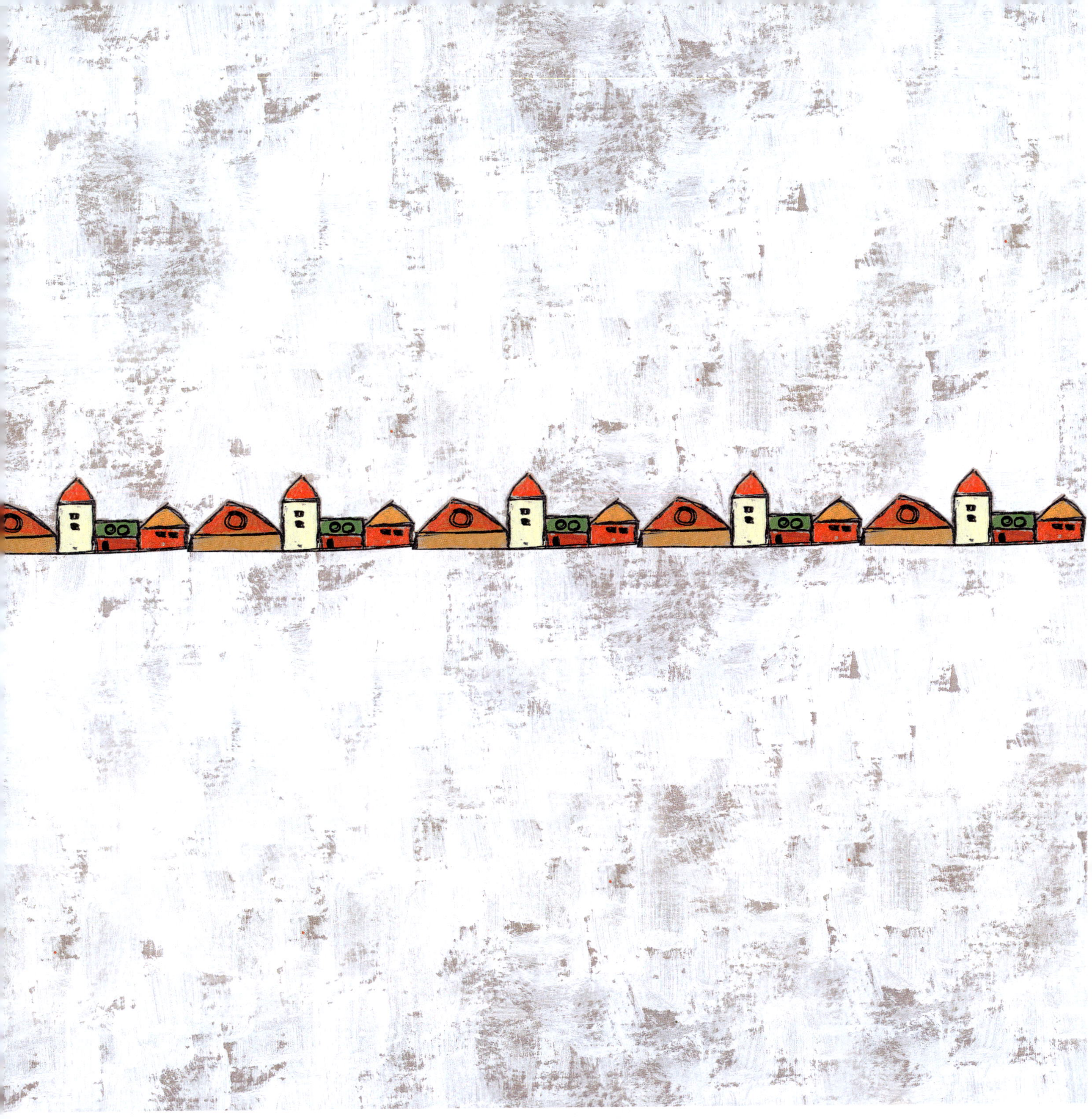

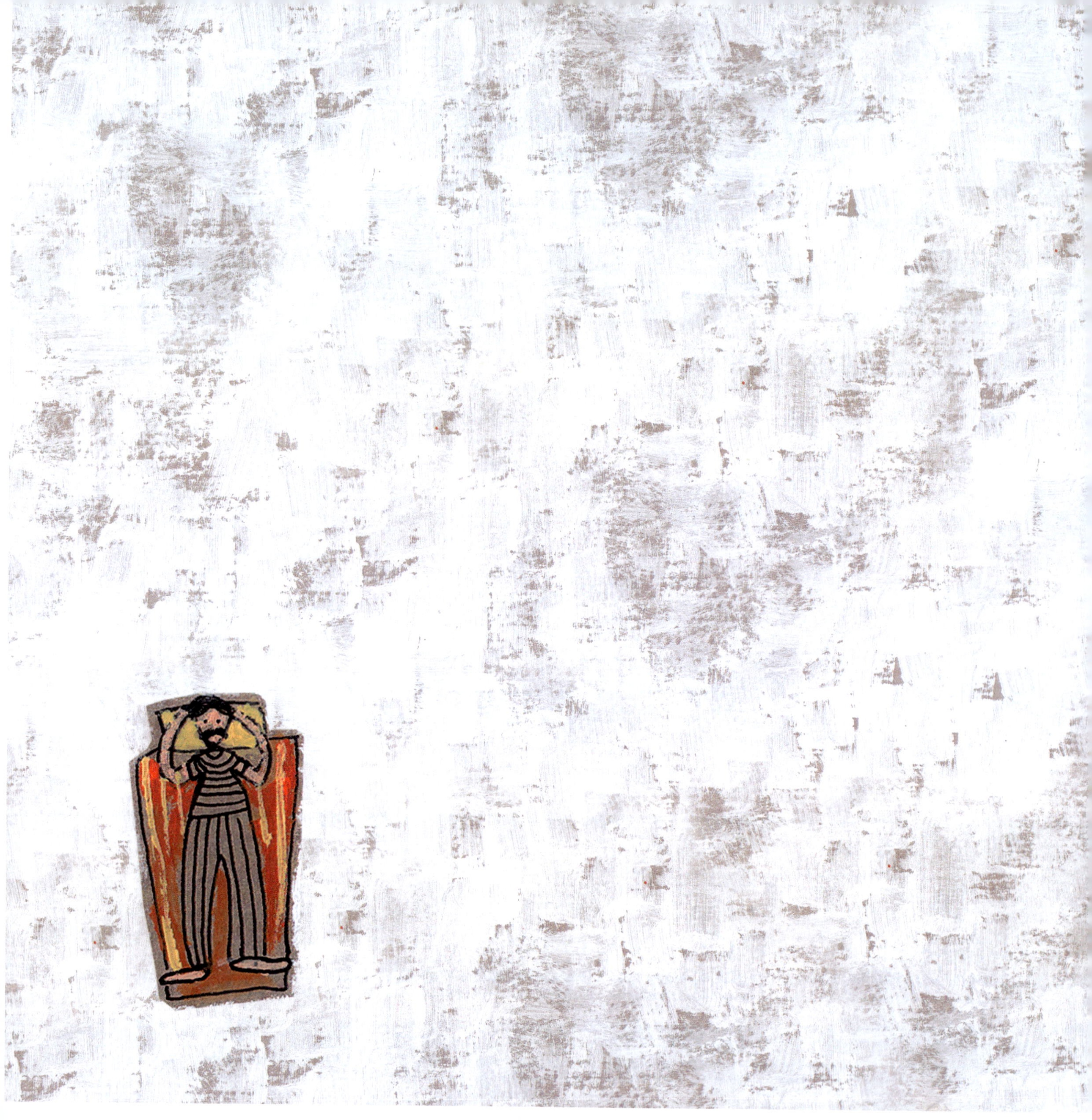

9 781763 818460

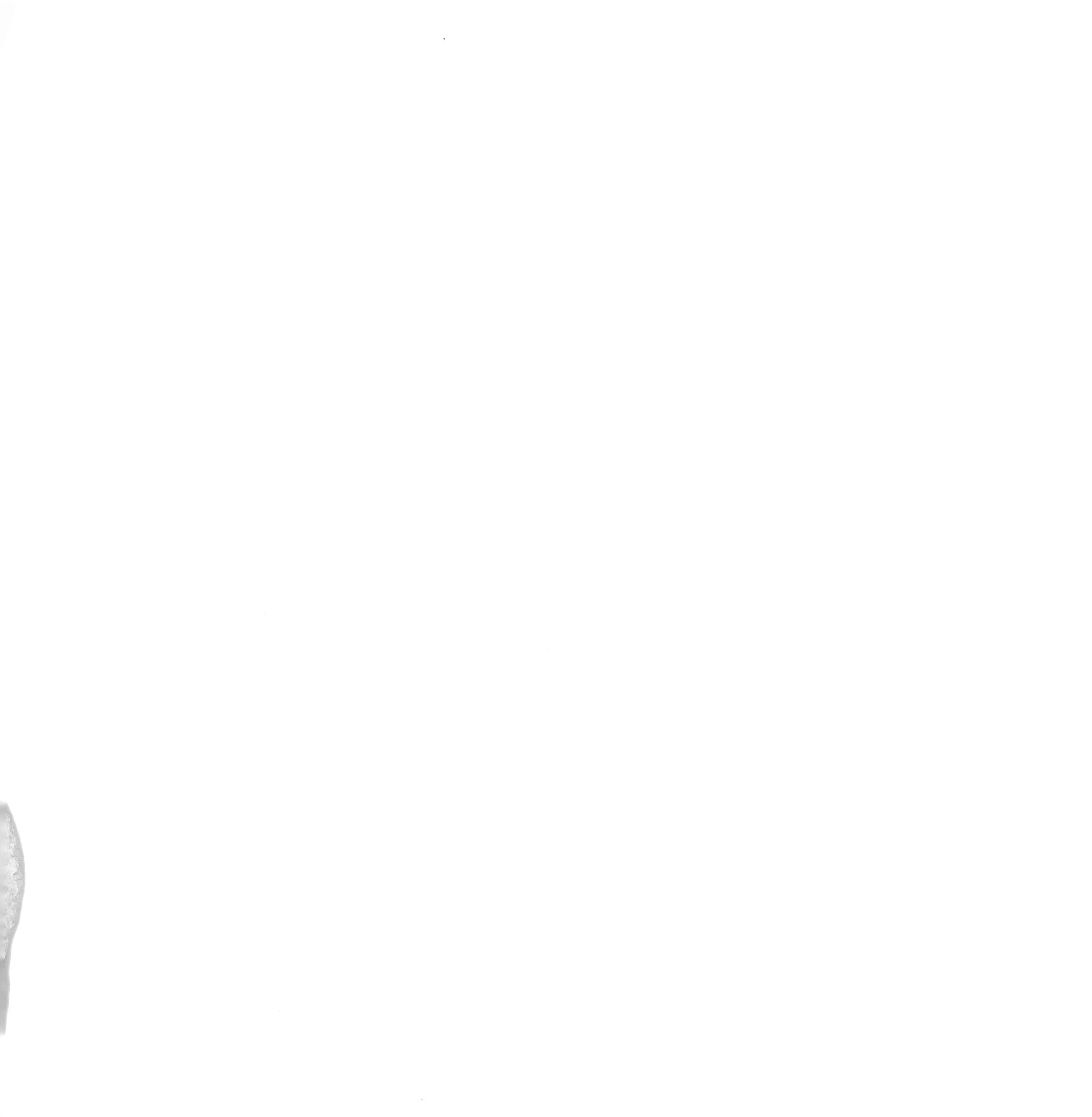